Courtesies in The Gulf Area

Cour
in Th
Ar

**A DICTIONARY OF
COLLOQUIAL PHRASE
AND USAGE**

esies
Gulf
a

Sir Donald Hawley

STACEY
INTERNATIONAL

Contents

Courtesies in The Gulf Area

by Sir Donald Hawley

Other books by the same author
The Trucial States
Courtesies in the Trucial States
Oman and its Renaissance
Sandtracks in the Sudan

First published by Stacey International 1978
Revised edition 1998

British Library Cataloguing-in-Publication Data
A catalogue record for this book is available from the British Library.

Stacey International
128 Kensington Church Street
London W8 4BH
Fax: (44) 171 792 9288

ISBN 1 900988 03 8

Design by Anthony Nelthorpe
Cover design by Josephine Cotter
Set in Times New Roman and Naskh by Aurora Press Limited, Wimbledon, London
Printed at Oriental Press, Dubai, U.A.E.

SIR DONALD HAWLEY has long experience as a scholar of the Gulf Area and this work follows his well-known publications, *Oman and its Renaissance*, *The Trucial States*, *Courtesies in the Trucial States* and *Sandtracks in the Sudan*.

Trained as a Barrister-at-Law, he worked with the Sudan Government (1944-5) and thereafter served with H.M. Diplomatic Service, as Political Agent in Dubai (1958-61) and in Cairo, Lagos and Baghdad. He was a Visiting Fellow to the Department of Geography, Durham University, 1967-68. Sir Donald was Britain's first Ambassador to Oman (1971-75) and was British High Commissioner in Malaysia (1977-1981). Since retirement he has maintained contact with the Gulf area. He has been awarded with the honorary degrees of D.Litt. (Reading) and D.C.L. (Durham).

Foreword

DONALD HAWLEY and I first met nearly twenty years ago waiting at Sharjah for a 'plane to take us to Buraimi. As I recall the 'plane had its side door open during the flight and, since it was high summer, we were duly grateful for this impromptu ventilation system. Within a day or two both of us had spoken to Sheikh Zayid; then governor of Al-'Ayn oasis for his brother, now ruler of Abu Dhabi and president of the United Arab Emirates.

Some of his experience in this area Donald Hawley put into his books *Courtesies in the Trucial States,* published in 1965, and *The Trucial States,* which came out five years later.

Almost all of his distinguished career has been in Arab countries, but both he and I have a particular affection for Oman where he recently served as our Ambassador, and where I have done a good deal of research work over many years on Arabic and on the Modern South Arabian languages.

T.M. Johnstone. SCHOOL OF ORIENTAL AND AFRICAN STUDIES

Preface

THIS REVISED EDITION of my book has been produced in response to suggestions that a new edition would be welcome. A few changes have been made and it is hoped that it may be of interest to a wider public, though primarily intended for those who know some Arabic.

Modes of travel, the speed of life, changed habits and the growth of modern bureaucracies and businesses and the more prevalent use of English have affected attitudes and manners. However, although a modern classical *lingua franca* is now more widely spoken and although words in general use have changed somewhat, the greetings, farewells, condolences and everyday courtesies are used in much the same way as in the past. They remain current usage generally in Saudi Arabia as well as the Gulf states. There are, of course, specific local differences, but the whole of this part of Arabia has long established traditions of its own and, despite the great development of recent years, it still retains an individuality in speech and customs.

This book both in its original form and as a revised edition owes something to my earlier book *Courtesies in the Trucial States*. The Omani proverbs – which are not confined to Oman – have largely been taken from an article on "Omanee Proverbs" by Lt Col. A.S.G Jayaker, written in 1903. I also gained valuable ideas from *The Short Vocabularies of Omani Arabic* prepared by Mr Hugh Leach. I remain much indebted to the late Professor Tom Johnstone of the School of Oriental and African Studies, London University, for reading the manuscript, making many valuable suggestions and reading the proofs. I also remain very grateful to Mr Khalfan Nasir, Sir John Moberly, Mr Leslie McLoughlin, Sir Gawain Bell, Mr Hassan Salim, Mrs Akram Qursha, Sir Terence Clark and Mr David Tatham for their useful comments.

I must, however, absolve all of those who helped me so much from any responsibility for the final version, on which I had to take the ultimate decisions myself.

Donald Hawley
1998

Notes on Transliteration

No two people ever agree on the way Arabic should be rendered in Latin letters. The aim in this book has been to make transliteration as simple as possible. Broadly the idea has been that the transliteration should be such that one can read the relevant line as English and find oneself very near to the Arabic pronunciation. The stroke over a letter implies a lengthening and the correct pronunciation of the vowels shown below is:

ā as in pa
ī as in seen
ū as in soon
ō as in own (*as in N. English or Scots*)
ei as in hay (*as in N. English or Scots*)

One of the difficulties, however, in transliterating Arabic is the presence in the Arabic alphabet of more than one form of certain letters. The most significant of these which can cause difficulty have been rendered as follows with, rather oversimplified, suggestions for pronunciation for those unacquainted with the Arabic script.

Arabic	*English transliteration*	*pronounce as*
د	*d*	day
ض	*ḍ*	door (velarised *viz* soft and rounded)
ذ	*dh*	other
س	*s*	sat
ص	*ṣ*	saw (soft and rounded)
ت	*t*	take
ط	*ṭ*	tor (soft and rounded)
ظ	*ṭh*	though (soft and rounded)
ث	*th*	thief

حـ	*ḥ*	hard (guttural)
هـ	*h*	home (soft)
ك	*k*	kale
خـ	*kh*	loch
غ	*gh*	a French "r"
جـ	*j*	George
ق	*g*	gale

Pronunciation in the area is by no means uniform and in Oman for instance one finds the hard جـ(*gīm* or *jīm*) and the soft in different areas of the country. The same applies to ك (*kaf*) and to the length given to the أ (*alif*). In deciding on the transliteration I have attempted to follow the most general pronunciation in the area. The Arabic letter *qaf* (ق) has been transliterated *g*. This is a near approximation to the actual pronunciation in some areas. However, in some parts this letter is softened and becomes a *j*, *eg muwaffijīn*. The Arabic letter ك (*kaf*) has been rendered as *k*. It is pronounced correctly in this hard fashion in most of Oman. However, in many other parts of Arabia, including the Union of Arab Emirates, the common way of pronouncing it is *ch* as in "chafe", which is exactly how they pronounce the Arabic كيف (*keif*)! The Arabic letter *ain* (ع) has been rendered with an apostrophe thus ('), but the Arabic *hamza* has been omitted in the transliteration. Wherever possible I have tried to write and spell the Arabic text in the approved literary style and to confine eccentricities of pronunciation *etc* to the transliteration; but this is primarily a collection of colloquial expressions, and, where a search for an acceptable classical equivalent would have led too far from what is in fact said, I have transliterated that into Arabic script. Although I am aware of not having been entirely consistent, I have veered in the transliteration towards the classical pronunciation in cases where pronunciation varies from area to area.

Chapter One
MANNERS IN GENERAL

THE TRADITIONAL courtesies which are exchanged in the Gulf are deeply rooted in the region's distinctive Islamic tradition. Nearly all the phrases used are related to the Almighty, just as they were in earlier European tradition. Both in the settled towns and villages and in the desert areas occupied by the Bedu tribes the exchange of greetings and courtesies plays a much more important part in people's lives than is now customary in Europe, except in the more remote country areas.

Consequently it is still usual, particularly in places away from the larger towns, to greet strangers and, if a stranger greets one, it is *de rigueur* to reply. Frequently one hails a passer-by from a considerable distance and local people often give the impression of shouting their greetings. The probable origin of these shouted greetings is the need for the Bedu to greet one another over considerable tracts of desert or for hillsmen to greet one another across the valleys. All in all the Arabs of this area are more demonstrative in their greetings than we are in the West and the elaborate courtesies which they exchange may seem flowery, stilted, exaggerated and certainly repetitive. Indeed a degree of repetition is almost essential to ordinary politeness.

The customary gesture of greeting is the *salaam* which is rather like a military salute and is normally given with the right hand; the left hand is used for unclean purposes. It is usual to shake hands – without any question of introduction – and on entering a place one may find oneself shaking hands with a considerable crowd of local people gathered together. Handshakes may be very prolonged and in some areas a host may continue to hold one's hand as he leads one into his house. There is no horror of physical contact such as there sometimes is in northern Europe. Hosts frequently greet their guests at the door and after a meal or a visit see them off by walking to the door or even the car with them.

There are certain rituals connected with giving and receiving hospitality which are still followed, particularly in places away from the capitals and in *majlises.* For instance, if one is invited by one's host, be he Ruler, Wali or Sheikh, to precede him in anything, eg to take coffee first, one should say *tafaḍḍal* to him several times before giving in to his expressed wish with good grace as his guest. Sometimes, however, important personages will eventually take food or coffee first, if they consider this right in accordance with the local rules of precedence.

When one calls on a Wali, a Sheikh or a private individual, one will normally be offered *qahwa* which is often a host's modest way of referring to a light meal known as *fuwāla. Qahwa* literally means coffee, but its meaning is very elastic and can refer to anything from a small cup or two of traditional coffee to a comparatively large meal. It may include tea, fruit of various sorts, wheat *(burk)* bread in large round pieces with honey, a light meat dish, dates, fizzy drinks, tea and *ḥalwa* which may appear in large lumps or, in the more elegant houses, in small individual dishes.

One should not hesitate to plunge one's right fingers into this delicacy. Sometimes the *qahwa* appears fairly soon after arrival but on other occasions it is called for by the host shouting *qahwa* just before it is time to take one's leave. Indeed on some occasions it is only called for after one has made the first move to depart. Sometimes rose-water and incense is served and the Omanis have a saying: "No staying on after the incense."

Although the universality of the Swiss and Japanese watch has changed attitudes in many parts, time is not always viewed in a European light. For instance the western maxim that "time is money" would be regarded as very crude and vulgar. Late arrival is, therefore, not necessarily to be attributed to discourtesy. It may stem from an indifference to time in the European sense or from a misunderstanding or confusion between "English" and "Arabic" time, which is reckoned from sunset. One very seldom sees an Arab from this part of the world showing signs of impatience even if he has to put up with long waits.

During the pleasantries stage of a conversation the topics may range over where the visitor has come from, how long he took, by what means he came, the weather and the health of the Sultan, Ruler, Walis, Sheikhs or mutual friends.

Europeans are frequently referred to by their surnames without the prefix of “mister”. This should not be misconstrued; it is common practice and tends to be a sign of friendship. In expressing admiration one may be supposed to be coveting something which one only wanted to admire and, if one is misguided enough to express admiration to one’s host of some article which could be given away as a gift, one may find oneself embarrassed by being presented with it.

The taking of photographs is a delicate matter. Normally men do not mind being photographed, though it is often better to ask if they have any objection particularly as there are areas where people definitely do not like it. It is preferable for men not to photograph women, but some local women do not object if they are photographed by European women, or even men, if they are asked first. It helps if the foreign lady can first enter into a little conversation.

In general the customs in the Gulf region are based on innate Arab courtesy and the warmth and friendliness of the people is remarkable and refreshing in an age which has in general become far from elegant.

Chapter Two
GREETINGS

General Greetings

THE USUAL greeting, which may sometimes also be used on leaving a party is:

السلام عليكم   Peace be upon you
as-salāmu 'aleikum

This is said just before or at the same time as a handshake, which may be prolonged for a considerable time in the case of old friends. Where the greeting is given to someone a little distance away it is usual at the same time to give a salute, (*salaam*). In some areas the people, on greeting one another, kiss on the nose, and sometimes the lips. There is no need to emulate them.

The reply to this is:

وعليكم السلام   On you be peace
wa 'aleikum as-salām

which is usually followed up with the question:

كيف حالك ؟ (بخير؟)   How are you? (singular) Well?
keif ḥālak? (bi-kheir?)

كيف حالكم ؟   How are you? (plural)
keif ḥālkum?

or

اشحالك ؟   How are you?
ish ḥālak?

The reply to this is always formal, whatever the true state of affairs and is:

الحمد لله – زين طيب او بخير *al-ḥamdu lillāh, zein (*or *ṭayyib* or *bi-kheir)*	Praise be to God. Well (singular)
	or
الحمد لله زينين (طيبين) *al-ḥamdu lillāh zeinīn* (or *ṭayyibīn*)	Praise be to God. Well (plural)
	or
زين (طيب) لله الحمد *zein* (*ṭayyib*). *lillāh al ḥamd*	Well. To God be the praise
	or
يسرك الحال *yasurrak al-ḥāl*	Well (lit: The condition would please you)
	or
يسروك *yasurrūk*	This (condition etc) would please you
	or
بنعمة *bi-ni'ma*	Well (lit: In a state of content)
	or
بنعمة الله *bi-ni'mat Allah*	By God's grace (well)

In Oman, people often reply:

بخير بوجود جلالة السلطان *bi-kheir bi-wujūd jalālat as-Sultān*	Good, since His Majesty the Sultan is there

Formal greetings are prolonged far beyond the normal practice in Europe, and either party may several times repeat the phrase:

كيف حالكم (كيف حالك) ؟ *keif ḥālkum?* (or *keif ḥālak*)	How are you?

A phrase which is used commonly in Iraq and other parts of the Gulf, but rather rarely in Oman is:

اشلونك (شلونك) ؟ *ish-lōnak* (*shlōnak*)	How are you? (lit: What is your colour? or condition?)

Suitable answers to this, which may also be used as words of welcome at any time during the preliminaries of the conversation are:

الله يعافيك (يعافيك) *Allah yu'āfīk* (or merely *yu'āfīk*)	May God grant you health
or	
عافاك (عافاكم) *'āfāk* (*'āfākum*)	May he (God) grant you health
or	
الله يحييك (يحييك) *Allah yuḥaiyīk* (or merely *yuḥaiyīk*) (sometimes pronounced *yḥaiyīk*)	May God give you life
or	
قدوم (وصول) مبارك *gudūm* (*wuṣūl*) *mubārak* (sometimes pronounced *mbārak*)	A blessed arrival
or	
حياك (او حياكم) الله *ḥayyāk* (or *ḥayyākum*) *Allah*	Welcome (lit: May God give you life)
or	
الله يسلمك (او سلامة الله) *Allah yusallimak* (sometimes pronounced *ysallimk* in Oman and *ysallmik* in the Gulf) (or *salāmat Allah*)	May God keep you safe
or	
اهلا وسهلا *ahlan wa sahlan*	Welcome (lit: [You have found] relations and easy going)

or

عساك طيب *'asāk ṭayyib*	I hope you are well

or

تستاهل الخير *tistāhil al-kheir*	You deserve good

or

مرحباً *marḥaba*	Welcome

or

يا مرحبا *yā marḥaba*	O welcome

or

بارك الله فيك *bārak Allāh fīk*	May God bless you

or

المعونة *al-ma'ūna*	You have arrived with God's help (lit: Help)
تفضل (اتفضل) معنا *tafaḍḍal* (*itfaḍḍal*) *ma'āna*	Please join us

or

قربوا *garribū* (sometimes pronounced *garrbu* in Oman and *girbu* in the Gulf)	Join us (lit: Come close)

or

اتقهووا *itgahwu*	Take coffee

or

غدفوا *ghadafu*	Come and join us

Sometimes people greet one on arrival by saying one of the following phrases:

وصلتوا *waṣaltū*	You have arrived (*ie* in safety)
or	
مشيتوا *masheitū* (sometimes pronounced *misheitu*)	You have finished your journey
or	
ماشين *mashīn*	You are travelling

The answer to this can be:

مواصل الله *muwāṣil Allah*	God has brought me here
or	
وصلت (ج وصلنا) الحمد لله *waṣalt* (pl. *waṣalna*) *al-ḥamdu lillah* (sometimes pronounced *wṣalt* or *wṣilt* in Oman)	I have arrived. Thanks be to God

After the formal part of the conversation is over, questions may be asked about the health of the other person's children and individual members of his family (or where both parties are female, the female members). For example:

كيف حال الأولاد (اوالعيال أوالفروخ او الجهال *keif ḥāl al-aulad?* (or *al-'iyāl* or *al-firūkh* or *al-juhāl*)	How are the children?
كيف حال الشيخ أحمد ؟ *keif ḥāl ash-Sheikh Aḥmad?*	How is Sheikh Ahmad?
كيف حال محمد؟ *keif ḥāl Muḥammad?*	How is Muhammad?

The reply to this is formal, namely:

الحمد لله زين (او طيب) *al-ḥamdu lillāh, zein* (or *ṭayyib*)	Praise be to God, well

or

يسلم عليك *yusallim 'aleik*	He greets you

In some parts of the area, it is usual to ask the following question quite early in the conversation:

شو العلوم ؟ *shu il-'ulūm?*	What news is there?
شيْ علوم ؟ *shi'ulūm?*	Is there any news?

The answer to this being:

ما شيْ علوم *mā shī 'ulūm*	There is no news (lit: nothing untoward)

or

العلوم زينة *al-'ulūm zeinah*	The news is good

or

خير *kheir*	Good

or

خير وسكون *kheir wa sukūn*	Good and quiet

or

كل شيْ هادئ *kull shī hādi*	Everything is quiet

In some parts of Oman:

حاشي *hashī*	Nothing

or

ما شـيء *mā shī*	Nothing
or	
سلامتك *salāmatak* (sometimes pronounced *salāmatik* (m) and *salāmatich* (f))	There is no news (lit: Your safety *or* well being)
or	
شيء علوم من جانبك ؟ *shī 'ulūm min jānibak?*	Is there any news on your side?

After the initial formal greetings, it is usual to ask about the actual state of affairs and the following phrases may be used:

كيف الحال ؟ *keif al-ḥāl?*	How are things?
or	
كيف الأحوال ؟ *keif al-aḥwāl?*	How are things?
or	
كيف الأمور؟ *keif al-umūr?*	How are matters?
كيف حال تواليكم ؟ (رباعكم) *keif ḥāl towālīkum? rubā'kum*	How are your people? (family)
or	
شو أخبار الدار؟ *shū akhbār ad-dār?*	What is the news of the area?

To these questions the true answer should be given and suitable answers according to circumstances are:

والله زين *wallāhi zein*	By God. Good
or	
والله موب زين *wallāhi mūb zein*	By God. Not good
or	

هـدوء *hudū*	Quiet
or	
سـكون *sukūn*	Quiet
or	
واجد (او وائد) زين *wājid (wāid) zein*	Very good
or	
الدار ساكنة *ad-dār sākina*	The area is quiet
or	
دارك ساكنة *dārak sākina*	It is your area and it is quiet
or	
من أحسن ما يرام *min aḥsan mā yurām*	As good as could be wished
or	
على ما يرام *'ala mā yurām*	All that could be wished

Sometimes one may convey greetings on behalf of someone else *eg*:

احمد يسلم عليك *Ahmad yusellim 'aleik*	Ahmad sends you greetings

Morning and Evening Greetings

The ordinary morning greeting is:

صباح الخير (او صبحك الله بالخير) *ṣabāḥ al-kheir (or ṣabbaḥak Allah bil-kheir)*	Good morning (or: May God grant you a good morning)

The reply may be to repeat the same greeting or to say:

صباح النور *ṣabāḥ an-nūr*	Good morning (lit: Morning of light)

Which may be followed with the question:

كيف أصبحت ؟ *keif aṣbaḥt?*	How are you this morning?

The reply to which is:

صبحك الله بالخير (الله صبحك بالخير) *ṣabbaḥak Allah bil-kheir* (*Allah yuṣabbiḥak bil-kheir*)	May God grant you a good morning

The ordinary evening greeting is:

مساء الخير *misā' il-kheir*	Good evening

To which the reply is:

مساء النور *misā' in-nūr*	May you have an evening of light
or	
مساك الله بالخير *massāk Allāh bil-kheir*	May God grant you a good evening
or	
الله يمسيك بالخير *Allah yumassīk bil-kheir*	May God grant you a good evening

The phrase (*misā' il-kheir*) is, however, appropriate at any time after the midday prayers and it is normal to use it on meeting someone who has just said his prayers, even though one saw him only a few minutes previously. It may also be used for "Good Night" but the following may be used as well:

مساك الله بالخير *massāk Allah bil-kheir*	May God grant you a good evening
تصبح على خير *tiṣbaḥ 'ala kheir*	Goodnight (lit: May you wake up well)

The answer to this is:

وانتم من أهل الخير And you are good people
wa antum min ahal al-kheir

or (simply)

وانتم من أهله And you are people (of good)
wa antum min ahalu

or

وانتم بخـير And may all be well with you
wa antum bi-kheir

Chapter Three
FAREWELLS

BEFORE SAYING good-bye to a person whom one has been visiting, it is usual to say:

استرخص *astarkhiṣ*	I wish to take my leave
or	
نترخص *nitarakhkhaṣ*	We'll take our leave
or	
من رخصتك *min rukhṣatak*	With your permission
or	
عن اذنك *'an idhnak*	With your leave

The host may not necessarily reply to this, but he may say:

تفضل *tafaḍḍal*	Consider yourself free to do so
or	
عزيز *'azīz*	(You are still) dear (to me)

The host may also say:

شرفتوا (او شرفتونا) *sharraftu* (*or sharraftūna*)	You have honoured us

The reply to which is:

تشرفت *tasharraft*	I have been honoured

Before final farewells a departing guest, or the host, will frequently say:

شئ خدمة ؟ شئ امارة ؟ *shī khidma? shī imāra?*	Is there any service I can perform? Any order I can execute?

or

شئ امارة حاجة ؟ *shī imāra ḥāja?*	Have you any order or anything?

or

فى امارة شئ ؟ *fī imāra shī?*	Is there any order at all?

To which the following reply is appropriate:

سلامتك *salāmatak*	No (lit: Your well being)

The reply to this is:

احسنت جزاكم الله بالخير *Aḥsant jazākum Allāh bil-kheir*	You are kind (No) May God reward you with goodness

The usual phrase used when bidding farewell is:

في امان الله *fī amān Illāh*	To God's protection (I commit you) (lit: In the protection of God)

The reply to this is:

في امان الكريم *fī amān il-karīm*	To the protection of the Generous One (God) (I commit you)
or	
في امان الله *fī amān Illāh*	To God's protection (I commit you)
or	
في وداعة الله *fī widā'at Allah*	In God's peace

An assiduous host may say to a departing guest:

سامحونا *sāmiḥūna*	We have not done enough for you (lit: Forgive us)

To this the reply is:

ما تقصر *mā tagaṣṣar*	You do not fall short
or	
ما قصرت *mā gaṣṣart*	You have not fallen short

It is usual to shake hands on bidding farewell, but if one is bidding farewell to a Wali or Sheikh it is usual to shake hands with him and his immediate entourage only, though one may say *fi Amān Illah* to the company at large. It is important, when bidding farewell, to shake hands with the senior person present first.

In towns the phrase, which is commonly used in other parts of the Middle East, is also used:

مع السلامة *ma' as-salāma*	Go in peace

If one has not visited a place for a long time, it is usual for the host, some time before the final farewell, to use some such phrase as:

نورت بيتنا *nawwart beitna*	You have brought light to our house

The guest replies to this:

بيتا معمورا *beitan ma'mūran*	Your house is established

To which the host may add the words:

كل سنة وكل حول *kull sana wa kull ḥōl*	(I hope to see you) each and every year

The guest may then say:

الله يجمعنا بالخير (على الخير) *Allah yajma'na bil-kheir*	(I hope) God is bringing us together again for good

It may be desired to convey greetings to persons who are not present at the meeting, and just before the final parting one may, as a guest, say:

سلم على (احمد) *sallim 'ala (Aḥmad)*	My greetings to (Ahmad)
or	
بلغ سلامي الى (احمد) *balligh salāmi ila (Aḥmad)*	Convey my greetings to (Ahmad)

The reply to which is:

الله يسلمك *Allah yusallimak*	May God grant you safety
or	
سلاما يبلغ *salāman yablugh*	Your greetings are conveyed

If a departing guest is setting out on a long journey or a dangerous venture of any sort, the following phrases may be used:

الله معكم (او وياكم) *Allah ma'kum (or wiyyākum)*	God be with you
or	
موفقين خير *muwaffagīn kheir*	May you be successful

The reply to this latter phrase is:

الله يوفق الجميع May God grant success to all
Allah yuwaffig al jamī'

When a Muslim mounts a camel or any other animal, or when he gets into a car (or indeed when he is about to embark on any venture) he will often say:

بسم الله In God's name
bismillāh

Chapter Four

CONVERSATION PIECES

THIS CHAPTER contains phrases and items of vocabulary of use when discussing a variety of topics.

Travellers

Following the formal greetings it is usual for a host to say to a guest who arrived after a long journey:

ان شاء الله ما تكلفت *in shā Allāh* (pronounced *in shā-llah*) *mā takallaft*	I hope that you have not been troubled
or	
ان شاء الله ما شئ تكليف *in shā-llah mā shī taklīf*	I hope you had no trouble

to which the answer is:

ابدا ما شئ كلافة (تكليف) *abadan. mā shī kalāfa* (*in shā-llah mā shī taklīf*)	Not at all. There has been no trouble
or	
ما تكلفت *mā takallaft*	No. I have not been troubled

Alternatively a person may say to another who has come back from a long journey:

معونـة *ma'ūna*	You have arrived with God's help (lit: Help)

to which the reply is:

الله يعينك *Allah yu'īnak*	May God help you

To a person who is setting out on a pilgrimage to Mecca it is usual to say:

ان شاء الله موفقين للحج *in shā-llah muwaffaqīn lil-ḥajj*	God will that your pilgrimage be successful

the answer to which is:

الله يوفق الجميع *Allah yuwaffig al jamī'*	May God grant success to all

When greeting a person who has returned from the pilgrimage one may say:

مبارك عليك الحج *mubārak 'aleik al-ḥajj*	(May) your pilgrimage (prove) blessed (to you)
حجاً مقبولا *ḥajjan magbūlan*	An acceptable pilgrimage (meaning: in God's eyes)
or	
حجاً مبروراً *ḥajjan mabrūran*	An acceptable and blessed pilgrimage

Muslims sometimes say:

حجاً مقبولاً وذنباً مغفوراً *ḥajjan magbūlan wa dhanban maghfūran*	An acceptable pilgrimage and sins forgiven

If asked when one is leaving a place or if volunteering the information. one may say:

(a)

باروح *b-arawiḥ*	I shall go (in the evening)
or (b)	
باسري *b-asri*	I shall go (in the night)

or (c)

با سرح I shall go (in the morning)
b-asraḥ

or (d) more generally:

اسير الحين I am going now
asīr al-ḥīn

This may provoke some such remark as:

موتبطي وائد You are not staying long
mū tabṭi wāid

or

ابطي شوي واتونس. استحب ارمس معاك(وياك). Stay a little and enjoy yourself. I would like to chat with you
ibṭi shweiy wa itwannas. Istaḥibb armis ma'āk (wiyyāk)

If one is in a hurry and one is offered coffee, it is better to accept it, if possible. However if there is some doubt as to how long it will take to come, one may say:

زاهب ؟ Is it ready?
Zāhib?

The reply may give one an indication as to how ready it is.

When one is ready to depart and wishes to ask whether the other members of the party are ready to proceed, one may say:

بارزين ؟ Are you ready?
bārizin?

If one wishes to enquire whether one is liable to get stuck in the mud *en route* one may say:

ان شاء الله ماشي تغريز في الدرب ؟ I hope there is no sticking *en route*?
in shā Allāh mā shī taghrīz fi-d-darb?

A host may reply to this:

معاك ربيع ؟ Have you a guide (or follower)?
ma'āk rabī'?

One may greet a traveller who is late with the phrase:

ان شاء الله ما غرزتو I hope you did not get stuck
in shā-llah mā gharaztu

or

ان شاء الله ما شئ تكليف I hope there was no difficulty
in shā-llah mā shī taklīf

General

Sometimes a person signifies a desire to have a general talk with one and may say:

نرمس شوي ؟ Shall we chat a little?
narmis shweiy?

or one may be asked to dine in the evening for the purpose of a chat and the host may say:

نتعشى سوى ونرمس We will dine together and chat
nit'ashsha sawa wa narmis

If one wishes to describe someone as a good talker one may say:

يرمس زين He talks well
yarmis zein

or

رمسته زينه His conversation is pleasant
ramsatu zeinah

or

هو رماس He is a (fine) speaker
huwa rammas

If one wishes to instruct someone else to call a third party to one's presence:

اذكر عليه Call him
idhkar 'aleih

Conversational Queries

If one wishes to enquire what something is:

ايش هذا ؟ What is this?
eish hādha?

or

شو هذا ؟ What is this?
shū hādha?

Or if one wishes to enquire about some event which has occurred:

شو صار؟ What happened?
shū ṣār?

or

متى صار؟ When did it happen?
mata ṣār?

or

متى اجاء ؟ When did he come?
mata ajā?

If one is slightly incredulous about a matter and wishes to know more:

كيف ؟ How (could it be)?
keif?

Or, if an answer to the reason for something is sought:

ليش ؟ Why?
leish?

Or if one wishes to know where someone is one may say:

هين محمد ؟ Where is Muhammad?
hein Muḥammad? (Omani usage)

or

وين محمد ؟ Where is Muhammad?
Wein Muḥammad? (Gulf usage)

Or if one wishes to enquire who has been with someone else:

من وياك ؟ Who is (was) with you?
min wiyyāk?

من وياه ؟ *min wiyyāhu?*	Who is with him?

Hawking

Hawking is in abeyance until the bustards return.
Some appropriate phrases were:

كيف القنص ؟ *keif al-ganaṣ?*	How is the hunting?

To this the reply would usually be:

القنص زين *al-ganaṣ zein*	The hunting is good

However sometimes a truthful answer was given rather than a conventional one and the subject was one of such interest that it would not be long before the actual state of the hunting was revealed. One might then ask about the factors which affect hunting:

الأمطار زينة ؟ *al-amṭār zeinah?*	Are the rains good?
or	
العشب زينة (مخضرة) ؟ *al-'ushb zeinah* (*mukhaḍḍrah*)?	Is the grass (on which the bustard feed) good (green)?

Other phrases are:

كم حبارى قنصتوا (حصلت اوحصلوا)؟ *kām ḥubāra ganaṣtū* (*ḥaṣṣalt or ḥaṣṣaltu*)?	How many bustard have you bagged?
or	
وين احسن قنص (او مقناص) ؟ *wein aḥsan ganaṣ* (*or magnāṣ*)?	Where is the best hunting?
من عنده احسن طير؟ *min 'anduh ahsan ṭeir?*	Who has the best bird (hawk)?

Shooting

Shooting is a popular sport for many people in addition to those in the armed services. One may ask a person if shooting appeals to him by saying:

تحب الرمي ؟ Do you like shooting?
taḥibb ar-rami?

If a person is a good shot, one may say:

يرمي زين He shoots well
yarmi zein

The Weather

As in England, the weather is talked about a great deal, and some of the phrases frequently used are:

الهوا زين اليوم The weather is good today
al hawa zein al-yōm

or

wājid (*wāid*) *ḥarr al-yōm* It is very hot today

or

واجد (وائد) ضباب اليوم It is very misty today
wājid (*wāid*) *ḍubāb al-yōm*

or

واجد (وائد) غبار اليوم It is very dusty today
wājid (*wāid*) *ghubār al-yōm*

or

رطوبه واجد (وائد) It is very humid
ruṭūba wājid (*wāid*)

or

هوا جاف هونا (هنى) It is very dry here
hawa jāf huna (in the Gulf, *hini*)

and

هوا شديد اليوم It is very windy today
hawa shadīd al-yōm

The Sea

Conversation on the coast naturally often turns to the sea and boats. Some of the following phrases may crop up:

طوفان واجد (وائد) *ṭōfān wājid* (*wāid*)	The wind is strong
or	
هوا زايد *hawa zāid*	There is too much wind
or	
سجى واجد (وائد) *saji wājid* (*wāid*)	It is a very high tide
or	
ثبر الحين *thabur al-ḥīn*	The tide is now going out
or	
الماي يسجى (يثبر) *al-māi yasji* (*yathbur*)	The tide is coming in (going out)
or	
البحر تارس *al-baḥr tāris*	The tide is coming in
or	
البحر نازل (هابط) *al-bahr nāzil* (*hābiṭ*)	The tide is going out
or	
هو في بر ديره (دبي) *huwa fi barr Deira* (*Dubai*)	He is on the Deira (Dubai) side (of the creek)
or	
الخور جميل *al-khōr jamīl*	The creek is beautiful
or	
يصيد السمك *yaṣīd as-samak*	He is fishing

Chapter Five

FEASTS AND FASTS

THE PRINCIPAL feasts observed are the Id al Fitr, which is the feast celebrating the end of Ramadan, the month of fasting, and the Id al Adha, which is celebrated on the tenth day of Dhu'l Hijja, the month of the pilgrimage, when it is customary for all Muslims to slaughter an animal—a sheep or a goat. The beginning of the Id is marked by the firing of a gun. The day may differ in the various States in the area, since its occurrence usually depends on the sighting of the new moon by two reliable local witnesses.

On these occasions it is usual to call on important people locally to express greetings. Halwa and other sweets are usually served with coffee. It is not necessary to stay for long at any one place but one should not leave before coffee is served and, in some cases, it will be necessary to wait until rose-water and incense are also brought. Although the Mulid an Nabi (The Prophet's Birthday) is a holiday, no special visits are usual.

The usual phrase to express greetings on the Id, is:

عيدكم مبارك او مبارك العيد *'īdukum mubārak or mubārak al-'īd*	May your Id be blessed

The reply to this is:

الله يبارك فيكم (او لكم) *Allah yubārik fīkum* (or sometimes *likum*)	May God bless you
or	
معيدين *mu'ayyidīn*	We are celebrating (the Id)
or	

بالعايدين *bil- āyīdīn*	Greetings of the Id
or	
بركات العيد *barakāt al-īd*	Blessings of the Id
or	
ايامك سعيدة *ayyāmak sa īda*	May your days be happy

After the initial greeting, one may say:

كل سنة وانت طيب *kull sana wa anta ṭayyib*	May you be well every year

And the other party may reply:

كل عام وانتم بخير *kull 'ām wa antum bi kheir*	May you too be well every year

A suitable written greeting for an Id is as follows:

بمناسبة عيد الفطر (الأضحى) المبارك اتقدم اليكم باخلص التهاني والتمنيات الطيبة ، اعاده الله عليكم سنين عديدة بالخير والبركات ، وختاما تفضلوا بقبول الاحترام ودمتم	After greetings and respects: On the occasion of the blessed Id al Fitr (al Adha) I offer you my sincerest congratulations and good wishes. May God bring you many years of good and blessings. Finally please accept my respects and may God preserve you.

A suitable written reply is as follows:

اشكركم شكرا جزيلا على تهانيكم الرقيقة متمنيا لكم عيدا سعيدا مقرونا باليمن والبركة ، وختاما تفضلوا بقبول فائق الاحترام	After greetings and respects: Thank you very much for your kind congratulations. Wishing you a happy Id full of happiness and blessings. Finally please accept my highest respects and may God preserve you.

At the beginning of the month of Ramadan, when Muslims fast between sunrise and sunset and when the firing of a gun signifies the time at which food may be taken, it is usual to say:

مبارك (او مبروك) عليكم شهر رمضان *mubārak* (*or mabrūk*) *'aleikum shahr Ramaḍān*	May the month of Ramadan be a blessed one for you

The reply to this is, as a rule:

الله يبارك فيكم *Allah yubārik fīkum*	May God bless you

When the fast is broken at sunset one may say:

يقبل الله صيامكم *yagbul Allah ṣiyāmkum*	May God accept your fasting

The Shia community observes the 10th Muharram as a day of mourning. This was the day on which in 680 AD (62 Hijra) the battle of Kerbala was fought, when Hussein ibn Ali, the Prophet's son-in-law, and the sole surviving grandson of the Prophet, was killed. The cause of the battle was a dispute over the Caliphate, and the Shias believe that Hussein was the true Caliph. It is, therefore, appropriate to say on that day to a person, who is known to belong to that community, one of the phrases used to express condolences:

احسن الله عزاكم *aḥsan Allāh 'azākum*	May God grant you solace
or	
عظم الله اجركم *'atḥam Allah ajrakum*	May God grant you great reward

Chapter Six

FAMILY OCCASIONS

Marriage

ON THE occasion of a marriage one may say:

مبروك الزواج *mabrūk az-zawāj*	May the marriage be blessed

or

الله يبارك بك (او به) بالزواج *Allah yubārik bik* (*or bih*) *biz-zawāj*	May God bless your (or his) wedding

or

بالرفاه والبنين *bir-rafāh wal-banīn*	(I wish you) prosperity and children

or

نهنئكم بالزواج *nuhannīkum biz-zawāj*	We congratulate you on the marriage

or

بكرك ولد *bikrak walad*	May your first-born be a boy (Bedu usage)

The reply to which is:

الله يبارك فيكم (فيك) *Allah yubārik fīkum*	May God bless you

The exchange may be followed up with the words:

الله يرزقكم ولد مبروك *Allah yarzagkum walad mabrūk*	May God enrich you with a blessed son

or

بيتا مبروكا May the house be blessed
beitan mabrūkan

The reply to which is:

الله يبارك فيكم God bless you
Allah yubārik fīkum

Births

On the birth of a child the father may be congratulated thus:

مبروك عليك الميلاد Congratulations on the birth
mabrūk 'aleik al-mīlād

or

مبروك بالمولود الجديد Congratulations on the new child
mabrūk bil mawlūd al-yadīd

The answer to which is:

الله يبارك فيكم God bless you
Allah yubārik fīkum

As in other parts of the Arab world, a father is much more delighted by the birth of a son than the birth of a daughter. If the father shows signs of disappointment that a daughter, rather than a son, has been born one may say:

الثاني ان شاء الله ولد If God wills, the next one will be a boy
al-thāni in shā Allah walad

or

البنت علامة الخير *al-bint 'alāmat al-kheir*	A girl is a sign of good

or

خيركم من بكر ببنت *kheirkum man bakar bi bint*	The best of you is he who produces a girl first

Chapter Seven

CONDOLENCES

ON HEARING of a death, it is usual to say:

الله يرحمه ويغفر له *Allah yarḥamuh wa yaghfir luh*	May God pardon and forgive him (the dead man)
or	
الله يحله (ويبيحه ويرحمه) *Allah yaḥillu (wa yabīḥu wa yarḥamu)*	May God release him (and pardon him)
or	
انا لله وانا اليه راجعون *innā lillāh wa innā ileihi rāji'ūn*	We all belong to God and are returning to him
or	
الله يغفر ذنوبه *Allah yaghfir dhunūbu*	May God forgive his sins
or	
الله كريم *Allah karīm*	God is generous

There is no need to respond to this, but the following reply may be used:

الدوام والبقاء لله *ad-dawām wa-l biqā lillāh*	Eternity and existence is God's

The following expressions of sympathy are appropriate when one meets a relative or close friend of the deceased:

احسن الله عزاءكم *aḥsan Allāh 'azākum*	May God grant you solace
or	

عظم الله اجركم *'adhạm Allah ajrakum*	May God grant you great reward

It is the custom in some areas, particularly in the Union of Arab Emirates, to kiss the relative or friend addressed on the nose. However, other people should merely shake hands at the same time saying one of the phrases given above. The response to an oral expression of sympathy is:

الدوام لله *ad-dawām lillah*	Eternity is God's

A suitable letter of condolence is:

تأثرت غاية التأثر لنبأ وفاة المغفور له (لها) . . . واني لاعرب لكم عن اخلص التعزية القلبية واصدق المواساة في هذا المصاب الفادح وتغمد الله الفقيد بواسع رحمته والهمكم جميل الصبر ، وختاما تفضلوا بقبول فائق الاحترام ودمتم	After greetings and respects: I have heard with the greatest regret of the death of . . . I express to you my sincere and heartfelt condolence and deep sympathy in this terrible loss. May God keep the deceased in his ample pity and inspire you with fortitude. Finally, please accept my highest respects and may God preserve you.

A suitable letter in reply to a letter of condolence is:

بعد التحية والاحترام ، اشكركم جدا على تعازيكم الرقيقة بمناسبة وفاة المغفور له . . . داعيا المولى ان يتغمده برحمته وغفرانه انه سميع مجيب ، وختاما تفضلوا بقبول فائق الاحترام ودمتم	After greetings and respects: Thank you very much for your kind condolences on the occasion of the death of . . . and I ask God to be merciful to him and grant him forgiveness, for He is the listener, and the answerer. Finally, please accept my highest respects and may God preserve you.

Chapter Eight

EVERYDAY COURTESIES

THERE IS a word which has many uses and which is very commonly used. It can be used to welcome guests into the house, to urge them to precede one, to ask them to take their coffee before one, to ask them to sit down and make themselves comfortable, to invite them to come to the dinner or lunch table, or to make themselves at ease in any way.

تفضل Be at your ease (Be so good)
tafaḍḍal

If one wishes to say "please", it is usual to use one of the following phrases:

من فضلك Please (lit: Of your goodness)
min faḍlak

or

ارجوك I beg you
arjūk

If one wishes to beg another's pardon or to say "excuse me", it is usual to say:

اسمح لي Forgive me
ismaḥ lī

or

ما علي Do not (impute anything) against me
mā 'aleiy

or

كلفناك I have put you to trouble
kallafnāk

The reply to which may be:

مسموح (معذور) *masmūḥ* (*ma'adhūr*)	You are pardoned

If one wishes to express forgiveness for some small injury done to one, the following expressions may be used:

ما عليه *mā 'aleih*	It does not matter
ما يخالف *mā yukhālif*	It does not matter
or	
لا بأس *lā bās*	There is no harm (done)

If one wishes to thank another, it is usual to say:

مشكور *mashkūr*	(You are) thanked
or	
اشكرك *ashkurak*	I thank you
or	
احسنت *aḥsant*	You are doing a good thing (hence "thanks")

The reply to which is:

عفوا (العفوا) *'afwan* (*al-'afu*)	It is nothing
or	
مشكور فضلك *mashkūr faḍlak*	Your goodness is thanked
or	
هذا من احسانك *hādha min iḥsānak*	This is done to your goodness
or	

(هذا) من طيبك This is done to your goodness
(hādha) min ṭībak

To this the following reply may be given:

وانت اطيب You are better
wa anta aṭyab

If one wishes to tell another person not to trouble, one should say:

لا (ما) تتكلف Do not trouble
lā (mā) (tetakallaf)

If one is about to express disagreement with anyone, it is usual to precede whatever one is about to say with the words:

الله يسلمك May God save you
Allah yusallimak

If, however, the person addressed is the Sultan, a Ruler, or a very prominent person, one should say:

الله يطول عمرك May God prolong your life
Allah yuṭawwil 'umrak

or

طول عمرك (May God) prolong your life
ṭawwal 'umrak

A polite way of saying "No" is:

سلامتك Your safety
salāmatak

The usual words used to express assent are:

نعم Yes
na 'am

or

عدل That is correct
'adl

or

زين Good (*ie*: all right)
zein

or

يستوي It could be
yistuwi

or

لا بأس There is no objection
lā bās

It frequently happens that a subordinate, if told to go and do some job, will say:

ان شاء اللّة If God wills
in shā-llah

This is in no way a sign of disrespect and this phrase is used before any statement of future intention. Alternatively he may say:

حي والله I am alive by God (to serve you)
ḥayy wallah

or

لبيك At your service
labbeik

If one sees or hears that a friend has shaved or taken a bath, one may say to him:

نعيما You are at ease
na 'īman

The reply to this is:

الله ينعم عليك May God make you at ease
Allah yan 'im 'aleik

If one sees a friend wearing new clothes (other than on an Id day) one can say:

ملبوس العافية (You are) wearing (new) clothes
malbūs al-'āfiya and (may God give you) health too

After having drunk a glass of water or a soft drink (but not coffee), one may say:

هنيئا *haniyān*	I hope you enjoyed it

The reply to this is:

الله يهنيك *Allah yuhannīk*	May God give you joy

However *hanīyan* may be used by a coffee bearer after one has taken coffee as a sign of respect.

If one is offered water, but wishes someone else to take first, one may say:

تهنا *tahanna*	Be blessed

A subject may sometimes be concluded by saying:

على كل حال *'ala kull ḥāl*	At all events

If one is walking with an Arab through trees, in a garden or in woody country, he will always hold a bough, which may be spiky and dangerous, long enough to indicate it clearly, if he does not actually hold it back for his guest—a courtesy without words.

Chapter Nine
FORMAL OCCASIONS

It is the custom to offer coffee to guests on a variety of occasions. When offered coffee by one's host's servant it is polite to ask the host to take the first cup though he will very likely insist that the guest accepts this. A Ruler's or Wali's servant will nearly always offer coffee to his master rather than the guest first. Both host and guest say to the other:

تفضل *tafaḍḍal*	Be so good

The matter may be ended by one party saying to the other:

ارجوك *arjūk*	I beseech you
or	
حلفت (اقسمت) *ḥalaft* (*agsamt*)	I have sworn (*ie* I have sworn you shall precede me)
or	
ما يصير *mā yaṣīr*	It cannot be

As the guest, one should eventually give in with good grace and take the first cup. Except on formal occasions, when there are a large number of people present, the coffee bearer will refill the cup as soon as it is empty. One should normally take two or three cups, though in some more remote places it may be more appropriate to drink up to four or five. If one wishes to signify that no more coffee should be offered, the proper method is to shake the cup and say:

بس *bas*	Enough

But in Oman one may still be offered yet one more.

If one has been invited to a lunch or dinner, the host will rise and say, as soon as it is ready:

تفضل *tafaḍḍal*	Be so good

There is no need to reply to this, though one may use the same phrase to beg one's host to precede one to the meal. Before the meal it is usual for the host to offer one soap and water to wash one's hands, but normally all that is required of one is that the water be allowed to be poured from the kettle over the right hand.

Before actually eating, the host will usually say to the guest:

تفضل *tafaḍḍal*	Help yourself (Be at your ease and eat)
or	
سم *samm*	Lit: "Name God"

For Muslims before they start to eat frequently say:

بسم الله *bismillāh*	In God's name

Food is sometimes served on the floor and sometimes at table. When on the floor one should adopt a comfortable posture, and the only fixed rule is that one should not point the soles of the feet at anyone. This is considered very impolite, as amongst Arabs it is thought either to be a deliberate insult or a sign of great pride.

Custom varies on the amount of conversation there is at mealtime: but on the whole it is a time for eating rather than speaking and, if there are long silences, it does not mean that the party is a failure.

One should eat when possible with the right hand, and one should never dip one's left hand into the piled rice or any of the communal dishes. However, it is quite permissible to use the left hand for peeling fruit which one is going to eat oneself. There is no fear of one's being offered the sheep's eye, except possibly as a joke.

When one has finished eating one merely sits back. The host may press further pieces of meat or other food on one. It is polite to take a little more; but, when one has quite finished, it is usual to say:

والله اكلت By God I have eaten
wallāhi akalt

or

شبعت I am satisfied (I've had enough)
shiba't

or

هذا واجد كثير This is (too) much
hadha wājid kathīr

especially if one's host has said:

ما اكلت You've eaten nothing
mā akalt

In some places coffee, and sometimes tea as well, is served in the *majlis* after a meal. One should not leave until the coffee has been served to all those present. In some cases incense and rose-water are offered, but it is not necessary to wait for these unless one knows that they are coming. If they have not been offered shortly after the coffee, one may take leave, but if the host says that the incense and rose-water are coming, it is necessary to wait until they have been offered. When incense is offered one wafts the smoke into the nostrils and into the beard – if one is blessed with one – with a sweep of the hand. Rose-water is usually poured over the hand and it may then be applied *ad lib* to face, forehead or neck. However, it is sometimes poured over the head, and one may restrain a servant from drenching one too heavily by saying:

بس *bas* — Enough

Before leaving one's host, it is usual to say:

استرخص *astarkhiṣ* — I would like to take my leave

The host may not necessarily reply to this, but he may say:

تفضل *tafaḍḍal* — Consider yourself free to do so

or

عزيز *'azīz* — (You are still) dear (to me)

It is not usual to thank the host for the meal which he has offered, though one may say before leaving:

اكرمك (او اكرمكم) الله *akramak* (*or akramkum*) *Allah* — God will repay your kindness

or

زاد فضلك *zād faḍlak* — May God increase your kindness

or

انعم الله عليك *an'im Allah 'aleik* — May God bless you

or

نعمة دائمة *ni'ma dāima* — May you have perpetual well-being

or

سفرة دائمة *sufra dāima* — A perpetual feast (lit: table)

To which the host may reply:

هناء والعافية *hana wā-l-'āfiya* — Joy and health (be yours)

In the towns it is usual to thank one's host:

مشكور You are thanked
mashkūr

or

اشكرك I thank you
ashkurak

After this, normal farewells are said.

Chapter Ten

GOOD NEWS, BAD NEWS AND ILLNESS

If a person is the bearer of good news, it is usual for him to say to the person addressed:

بشارة Good news
bishāra

or

ابشرك I have some good news for you
ubashshirak

The answer to this is:

عسى خير (عسى بشرى خير) I hope it is good (news)
'asa kheir (*or 'asa bushra kheir*')

After that, the person bringing the good news explains precisely what it is, whether it be the birth of a child, the arrival of a ship, the safe arrival of an overdue car or traveller or any other good news.

If one hears of some disaster or misfortune having occurred to someone, the following phrases may be used:

ما يستاهل ، الله يخلف عليه He does not deserve it. May God make good his loss
mā yistāhil. Allah yakhlif 'aleih

or

رب العالمين كريم The Lord of the worlds is merciful
rabb il 'alamein karīm

or

طيب ان شاء الله All will be well, if God wills
ṭayyib, in shā-llah

or

ان شاء الله خير All will be well, if God wills
in shā-llah kheir

or

الله يعطيه الصحة والعافية *Allah ya'tīh as-ṣaḥḥa wa-l-'āfiya*	May God give him health and well-being

or

نتمنى له العافية *nitmanna lihu-l-'āfiya*	We wish for his health

or

الله يسلمه (يسلمك) من الشر *Allah yusallimu* (or *yusallimak*, in the case of a person who has suffered the misfortune himself) *min ash-sharr*	May God save him (or you) from evil

or

الله يحفظه من الشر *Allah yaḥfaṭhu min ash-sharr*	May God protect him from evil

The answer to the first phrase is:

الله يخلف عليك *Allah yakhlif 'aleik*	May God make good your loss

The answer to the last phrase is:

الحافظ الله *al-ḥāfiṭh Allah*	God is the protector

In all other cases, the phrases may be answered by:

الله يسلمك *Allah yusallimak*	May God save you

Any of the phrases set out above may be used also in the case of hearing that someone is seriously ill. In addition, the following phrase may be used:

ما يشوف الشر ان شاء الله *mā yashūf ash-sharr in shā-llah*	He will see no evil if God wills

or

ان شاء الله ما يرى باءس *in shā-llah mā yara bās*	If God wills he will see no evil

Visiting the sick is much appreciated and it is appropriate to say to a sick person:

طيب ان شاء الله You will get well, if God wills
ṭayyib, in shā-llah

or

ما تشوف الشر ان شاء الله You will see no evil, if God wills
ma tashūf ash-sharr, in shā-llah

or

ان شاء الله ما ترون باس If God wills, you will see no evil
in shā-llah mā tarūn bās

After recovery, the invalid may be greeted with:

ان شاء الله اهون I hope you are better
in shā-llah ahwan

or

الحمد لله على السلامة Praise be to God for safety
al-ḥamdu lillāh 'ala as-salāma

To which the reply is:

الله يسلمك May God save you
Allah yusallimak

On meeting someone who has had a narrow escape or had a difficult journey one may say:

تستاهل السلامة You deserve to be safe
tastāhil as-salāma

or

سالم من الشر You are saved from evil
sālim min ash-sharr

Likewise, if one hears from a relative or a friend that a mutual friend has had a narrow escape, one may say:

يستاهل السلامة He deserves to be safe
yistāhil as-salāma

The answer to all these phrases is:

الله يسلمك (او يسلمكم) May God save you
Allāh yusallimak (or *yusallimkum*)

If one hears of some general disaster, in which people have been killed or injured (such as a natural disaster like an earthquake), one may say:

امر الله (It is) God's order
amr Allah

or

قضاء وقدر It is fate and destiny
gaḍā wa gadr

The reply to which is:

أمنت بالله I believe in God
āmantu billāh

If some untoward event happens in one's presence, *eg* someone tripping up or falling, one may say:

يا ساتر يسترك O Protector, may he protect you
ya sātir yastūrak

or

سلمت You are safe
silimt

or

سلامات Safety!
salāmāt!

or

الله God!
Allah!

Chapter Eleven

ASTONISHMENT AND ADMIRATION

ON HEARING of some strange or unexpected event, some odd story or out-of-the way fact, one may say:

ما يستوي — It could not be
mā yistuwi

or

صح ؟ — Is it really true?
ṣaḥḥ?

or

سبحان الله — Praise be to God
subḥān Allāh

or

اعوذ بالله من الشر (او من الشيطان) — I seek God's protection (from evil or from the devil)!
a'ūdhu billāhi (*min ash-sharr* or *min ash-sheiṭān*)!

(This is the preface to any reading from the Qur'an but the phrase is used, sometimes jokingly, as an insurance, somewhat as we use "touch wood", the idea being that by mentioning God's name the evil spirit will be warded off.)

or

هذه مصيبة — That is a catastrophe
hādhihi muṣība

or

استغفر الله — I ask God's pardon!
astaghfir Allāh!

Admiration may be expressed by saying with a suitable inflection of the voice:

زين Good
zein

or

مبروك Congratulations
mabrūk

or (*in some circumstances*)

اهنئكم I congratulate you
uhannīkum

or

ما شاء الله As God willed
mā shā-llah

or (*wishing success to a new enterprise or on a first visit to a new home*)

عامر ان شاء الله May it thrive, if God wills
'āmir in shā-llah

or

موفق ان شاء الله May it be successful
muwaffag in shā-llah

The reply is:

الله يوفق الجميع May God grant success to all
Allah yuwaffag al-jamī'

or (*in some places*)

آمين Amen
āmīn

Chapter Twelve

OMANI VOCABULARY

THE FOLLOWING is a list, taken a little at random, of words which are commonly used in Oman or other parts of the Gulf area but which may either not be used elsewhere or used in a different sense. Alternatively the normal Omani or Gulf word has in some cases been given if it is a less common form elsewhere. They are for the most part words or usages which someone who has learnt Arabic in other parts of the Arab world might be surprised to come across.

A

سلف (اسلاف)	*salaf* (*pl. aslāf*)	advance (of money)
عقب	*'ugub*	afterwards
طائرة	*ṭāira*	aircraft
سمح	*samaḥ*	allow
لوزة	*lōza*	almond
نوبـة	*nōba*	also
رسا	*risa*	anchor (*vb*)
عتيق	*'atīg*	ancient
متكدر	*mutakaddir*	angry (*adj*)
تكدر	*takaddir*	angry (to be: *vb*)
برز	*baraz*	appear (or sit) in court
عربان	*'arbān*	Arabs (kinsmen)
دبر	*dabbar*	arrange
بعـد	*ba'ad*	as well
دلال	*dallāl*	auctioneer

B

حمقان	*ḥamgān*	bad-tempered
سامان	*sāmān*	baggage

لحيـة	*liḥya*	beard
شبرية (شباري)	*shubrīya* (*pl. shabāri*)	bed
اهون	*ahwan*	better (after illness)
اشوى	*ashwa*	,, ,, ,,
عـود	*'ūd*	big
هايل	*hāil*	,,
دوربين	*durbīn*	binoculars (or telescope)
ملحف	*malḥaf,*	blanket
برنوس	*barnus*	,,
اعـور	*'awar*	blind; one-eyed (*adj*)
منجـور	*manjūr*	block (with pulleys from ship's rigging)
ديـة	*diya*	blood money
افتخر	*iftakhar*	boast (*vb*)
غـرز	*gharaz*	bogged (to get: *vb*)
مغـروز	*maghrūz*	bogged
طاسـة	*ṭāsa*	bowl (for washing hands)
مندوس (مناديس)	*mandūs* (*pl. manādīs*)	box (*eg* the brass studded type)
دستورية	*dastūrīya*	(small type)
فرخ (فروخ)	*farkh* (*pl. firūkh*)	boy (in Oman also a bastard)
بنجرة (بناجير)	*banjari* (*banājīr*)	bracelet
خبز	*khubz*	bread
ريوق	*riyūg*	breakfast (*n*)
تريّق	*tarayyag*	breakfast (to have: *vb*)
على الخلاصة	*'ala-l khalāṣa*	brief (in)
قرقرة ـ جرجرة	*gargara*	bumpiness
جـامبين	*jampīn*	,,
حبارة	*ḥubāra*	bustard
دكمة	*dukma*	button
جيب	*jeib*	,,

C

بعير	*ba'īr*	camel (male)
ناقة	*nāga*	,, (female)
مطية (مطايا)	*muṭīya (muṭāyā)*	camel (riding)
ركاب	*rukāb*	camels (riding)
بوش	*bōsh*	camels (collective)
جمال	*jimāl*	,, (male)
نوق	*nōg*	,, (female)
خرجة (خرج)	*kharja (khurūj)*	camel bag
ساحة	*sāḥa*	camel rug
شملة (شملات)	*shamla (shamlāt)*	,, ,,
مطرة (مطارات)	*muṭra (muṭārāt)*	canvas water bag
نوخذا (نواخذ)	*nōkhdha (nwākhidh)*	captain (of dhow)
سيارة	*sayyāra*	car
هيل	*heil*	cardamom
زولية (زوالي)	*zūlīya (zwāli)*	carpet
سنورة (سنانير)	*sannūra (sanānīr)*	cat
كهف	*kahf (pronounced kaf in Oman)*	cave
غوازي	*ghawāzi*	change (money) (*n*)
مندوس	*mandūs*	chest (studded, often called 'Kuwaiti')
جاهل (جهال)	*jāhil (juhhāl)*	child
دوك	*dūk*	clam
كراني	*karāni*	clerk
بشت (بشوت)	*bisht (bishūt)*	cloak
هدم (هدوم)	*hidim (or hidūm)*	clothes
قرنفل	*girunfil*	clove
بندر	*bandar*	coastal town
نارجيلة	*narjīla*	coconut
دلة (دلال)	*dalla (dilāl)*	coffee pot
مدلاة (مدالي)	*mudla (midāli)*	,, ,,
زكمة	*zukma*	cold (in the head)

زكام	*zukām*	cold (in the head)
زكمـان	*zukmān*	cold (to have a: *vb*)
مستريح	*mustarīḥ*	comfortable
قــر	*garr*	confess
استقر	*istagarr*	,,
بيت باليوز	*beit*	consulate
برابر	*barābir*	correct (*adj*)
برزة	*barza*	court room
بيت البرزة	*beit al-barza*	,, ,,
قبقب	*gubgub*	crab
جوشن	*gūshin*	,,
دشن	*dishin*	,,
ام الربيان	*umm ar-ribyān*	crayfish
شرخة	*sharkha*	,,
خارش بارش	*khārish bārish*	,,
غلة	*ghilla*	crop
كوب	*kūb*	cup
صرم (صروم)	*ṣirm* (*ṣirūm*)	cut (off a palm or a young palm: *n*)

D

رطب	*ruṭab*	dates
بسر	*bisir*	dates (dried)
اصم (صم)	*aṣamm* (*pl. ṣumm*)	deaf
تعطيل	*ta'aṭīl*	delay (*n*)
تحجر	*taḥajjar*	delayed (to be: *vb*)
طل	*ṭull*	dew
سوى	*sawwa*	do
مصري	*maṣri* (*lit: Egyptian. Originally it probably referred to an Egyptian type of donkey brought to the Arabian peninsula at some time in the past. It is not surprising that*	donkey

	this usage has tended to die with the advent of Egyptian schoolmasters)	
سائق	*sā'ig*	driver (also pilot)
غبار	*ghubār*	dust (*n*)
آل	*āl*	dynasty (*see also* family)

E

بدري	*badri*	early (morning)
ملحف	*malḥaf*	eiderdown
نقش	*ṅagash*	engrave
نقع	*naga'*	engraving (*eg* in plaster)
خوش	*khōsh*	excellent
تفجير	*tafjīr*	explosion

F

طاع	*ṭā'*	fall (*vb*)
آل	*Al*	family (usually ruling *eg* Al bu Said, Al Sabah, Al Khalifa, Al Thani, Al Nahhiyan)
ربع (رباعه)	*rab'* (*pl. ribā'a*)	family
فريق	*farīg*	,,
نول	*nōl*	fare (or fee)
قصر	*gaṣṣar*	fail
حس	*ḥass*	feel (to)
حواس	*ḥawāss*	feeling
ترس	*taras*	fill (*vb*)
بنديرة	*bandeira*	flag
رباعه	*ribā'a*	followers
غفل (عن)	*ghafal* (*'an*)	forget
حصيني	*ḥuṣeini*	fox
جثم	*jathm*	frost
غلة	*ghilla*	fruit

لبان	*lūban*	frankincense
متروس	*matrūs*	full

G

دشداشة (دشاديش)	*dishdāsha* (*dishādīsh*)	garment (long white)
دروازة	*darwāza*	gate
زطي (زطوط)	*zuṭṭi* (*zuṭūṭ*)	gipsy
قلاس	*galās*	glass (drinking)
كشمة	*kashma*	glasses
سار (يسير)	*sār* (*yasīr*)	go
خطف	*khaṭaf*	go by
برابر	*barābir*	good
فلاة	*falāh*	grazing ground
دعنة	*d'ana*	ground
زيتون	*zeitūn*	guava
سبلة	*sibla*	guest house
تفك (تفكان) (اوتفق)	*tafak* (*tafkān*) (*or tafag*)	gun
باروت	*bārūt*	gunpowder

H

حلوة	*ḥalwa*	'halwa'(Omani form of sweet)
مستانس	*mustānis*	happy
مصرّ	*muṣarr*	headdress (cloth wound round head)
عمامة	*imāma*	,,
شطفة	*shuṭfa*	headdress (traditional in Arabia)
غطرة	*ghuṭra*	headdress (soft cloth, white or patterned, worn with headrope– *see below*)
عقال	*'ugāl*	headrope
فواد (فودة)	*fu'ād* (*pl. fūda*)	heart
روحه	*rūḥu* (*pronounced so*	himself

	in Oman and rūḥa in the Gulf)	
جفرة	*jifra*	hole
عطلة	*'uṭla*	holiday (*see also* leave)
قنيص	*ganaṣ*	hunt (*vb*)
عوّر	*'awwar*	hurt (*vb*)
سافن	*sāfin*	hyrax
		I
مجهود	*majhūd*	ill
لزم	*lazam*	imprison
عود	*'ūd*	incense
مجمر	*majmar*	incense burner
شمج (شماج)	*shumaj* (*pl. shumāj*)	in-law
فرضة	*furḍa*	inspection hole (for *falaj*)
مكشوفة	*makshūfa*	,,
دسيس (دسس)	*dasīs* (*pl. dusus*)	intriguer
سمى	*samma*	invoke (the name of God)
باطن	*bāṭin*	inwardly
شئ	*shī*	is (there)
هست	*hast*	,,
ما (مو) شئ	*mā* (*mū*) *shī*	is not
ما هست	*mā hast*	,,
		J
فرضه	*furḍa*	jetty
جسر	*jusr*	,,
تـوا	*taww*	just now
		K
قلعة	*gal'a*	keep (of fort)
نمونة	*nimūna*	kind
ذبـح	*dhabaḥ*	kill (*vb*)
درى (ب)	*dara* (*bi*)	know

حاد	*ḥād*	know (*eg* the way)
اندل	*indall*	,,

L

سراج	*sirāj*	lamp
قنديل (قناديل)	*gandīl* (*ganādīl*)	,,
بتى	*butti*	,,
العام	*al-'ām*	last year
الحول	*al-ḥōl*	,,
خلاف	*khalāf*	later
عقب	*'ugub*	,,
رخصة	*rukhṣa*	leave (furlough)
يسار	*yasār*	left (opp. of right)
مكتوب	*maktūb*	letter
خـط	*khaṭṭ*	,,
قرطاس (قراطيس)	*gurṭās* (*garāṭīs*)	,,
لومى	*lūmi*	lime
سفرجل	*safarjil*	lime (sweet)
جت	*jatt*	lucerne
سامان	*sāmān*	luggage
اغراض	*aghrāḍ*	,,

M

همبا	*hamba*	mango
سماد	*samād*	manure
مجلس	*majlis*	majlis (room where men receive guests)
برزة	*barza*	,,
سوى (ترتيب)	*sawwa* (*tartīb*)	make (*eg* arrangements: *vb*)
يستوي	*yistuwi*	may be
برقع	*birga'*	mask (*n*)
جح	*yiḥḥ*	melon (water)
بطيخ	*baṭṭīkh*	melon (sweet)
سفد	*saffad*	mend (*vb*)

بشكار (بشاكير)	*bishkār* (*bishākīr*)	messenger
فراش	*farrāsh*	,,
رسول	*rasūl*	,,
مالي	*māli* (*Gulf*)	mine (my)
حالي	*hāli* (*Oman*)	,,
غوازي	*ghawāzi*	money
خريف	*kharīf*	monsoon
هاون	*hāwin*	mortar (*see also* pestle)
عقبة	*'agba*	mountain pass
واجد	*wājid*	much (also many)
وائد	*wāid*	,,
بروحي	*bi rūḥi*	myself (by)
مر	*murr*	myrrh

N

داير	*dāīr*	necessary
مول	*mūl*	never
بر	*barr*	,,
راس السنة	*rās as-sanah*	New Year
ما (مو) حد	*mā* (*mū*) *ḥad*	no one
موب	*mūb*	not
ما هست	*mā hast*	not much (many)
توا	*taww*	now
الحين	*al-ḥīn*	,,
تكليف	*taklīf*	nuisance

O

شاعبة	*shā'iba*	old man
عتيق	*'atīg*	old
دفلي	*difla*	oleander
حبن	*ḥibin*	,,
بطل	*baṭṭal*	open (*vb*)
بن سولع	*bin sōli'*	oryx
وضيحي	*wiḍeiḥi*	,,

محار	*maḥār*	oyster
صفد	*ṣafad*	,,

P

رنج	*runj*	paint (*n*)
قصر	*gaṣr*	palace
قرطاس	*girṭās*	paper (*n*)
حل تراب	*ḥall turāb*	paraffin
صفرد	*ṣifrid*	partridge
طوف	*ṭāf*	pass (*vb*)
عقبة	*'agba*	pass (of mountain)
فيفاي	*fīfāi*	pawpaw
راتب	*rātib*	pay (*n*)
لولو	*lūlū*	pearl
غوص	*ghōṣ*	pearling
قماش	*gumāsh*	pearls
اوادم	*awādim*	people (*n*)
يد هاون	*yid hāwin*	pestle (*see* mortar)
سفن	*safan*	,,
قبس	*qabas*	phosphorescence
شحبة	*shaḥba*	,,
عكس	*'akkas*	photograph (*vb*)
عكس	*'aks*	photograph (*n*)
مدواخ	*midwākh*	pipe (*n*)
جس	*juss*	plastic
ابو ريش	*abū rīsh*	porcupine
قد يكن	*gid yakūn*	possibly
مكحلة	*makḥala*	pot (or other silver container for *kohl*)
جحلة	*jaḥla*	pot (earthenware)
جدوية	*jadwīya*	,,
تلاحيق	*talaḥīg*	powder horn
متفخفخ	*mutfakhfakh*	proud
هست	*hast*	present (*adj*)

جـود	*jawwad*	pull (*vb*)
حط	*ḥuṭṭ*	put (*vb*)

R

حمق	*ḥamag*	rage (to be in)
مطر	*muṭar*	rain (*n*)
سيل	*sīl*	,,
تباق	*tubāg*	ray
بارز	*bāriz*	ready
زاهب	*zāhib*	,,
خاز	*khāz*	remove (*vb*)
صفد	*ṣaffad*	repair (*vb*)
نوخ	*nawwakh*	rest (while travelling: *vb*)
عيش	*'eish*	rice
يمين	*yamīn*	right (opp. of left)
عدل	*'adl*	right (correct) (*adj*)
خاتم	*khātim*	ring
رستة	*rasta*	road
خبيث	*khabīth*	rogue
حجرة	*ḥujra*	room
ما ورد	*māi ward*	rose-water
مرش	*murashsh*	rose-water sprinkler
فشكة	*fashka*	round (ammunition)
ربشة	*rabsha*	row or commotion

S

عقبة	*'agba*	saddle (of mountain)
نعال	*na'āl*	sandal
قطاة	*gaṭa*	sandgrouse
سفرية	*sufrīya*	saucepan
بدسية	*bi dussīya*	secretly
ترس	*tars*	shield (*n*)
جوتي (جواتي)	*jūti* (*juwati*)	shoe
روى	*rawwa*	show (*vb*)

روئية	*ru'ya*	sighting (*eg* of moon)
رقد	*ragad*	sleep (*vb*)
لين	*leiyin*	soft
حفارة	*ḥaffāra*	spade
كشمة	*kashma*	spectacles
كمشة (مقمشة)	*kamsha* (*magmasha*)	spoon (*n*)
قيل	*geiyil*	stay (during heat of the day or for lunch: *vb*)
بطى	*baṭa*	stay (*vb*)
غـرز	*gharaz*	stick (in mud: *vb*)
حصا	*ḥaṣa*	stone (*vb*)
طوفان	*ṭofān*	storm (*vb*)
سيده	*sīda*	straight ahead
بليد	*balīd*	stupid
سـد	*sadd*	suffice (*vb*)
قيظ	*gheiṭh*	summer
وارم	*wārim*	swollen

T

خاز	*khāz*	take away
ودى	*wadda*	,, ,,
نوبـة	*nōba*	time
فراغه	*farāgha*	time (opportunity)
قوطى	*gūṭi*	tin
ربعا	*rub'ān*	together
بجلى	*bujli*	torch
حمقان	*ḥamgān*	touchy
برج	*birj*	tower (*n*)
وطا	*waṭā*	tread (*vb*)
ربشة	*rabsha*	trouble (*n*)
بلبلة	*balbala*	,,
سحارة	*saḥāra*	trunk
حمسة	*ḥimisa*	turtle
غيلمة	*gheilma*	,,

نفق	*nifag*	tunnel (*n*)
منقاش	*mangāsh*	tweezers
نمونة	*nimūna*	type or kind

W

سيل	*seil*	wadi bed
جوز	*jōz*	walnut
سور	*sūr*	wall
بغى	*bagha*	want (*vb*)
طاسه	*ṭāsa*	washing bowl
ناطور	*nāṭūr*	watchman
فلج	*falaj*	water channel
نحـر	*naḥr*	,, ,,
طوى	*ṭuwi*	well (*n*)
مـو؟	*mū?*	what?
شو ؟	*shū?*	,,
ايش ؟	*eish?*	,,
بـر	*burr*	wheat
متى ؟	*mita?*	when?
يوم	*yōm*	when (*ie* the day when)
هين	*hein* (*Oman*)	,,
وين	*wein* (*elsewhere*)	where?
من	*min*	who?
فرخة الباب	*farkhat al-bāb*	wicket gate
طوفان	*ṭōfān*	wind(s)
دريشة	*darīsha*	window
ريح	*rīh*	,,
بادكير	*badkīr*	windtower
برقية	*bargīya*	wireless set
ساحر	*sāḥir*	witch (wizard)
ما يستوي	*mā yistuwi*	won't do

Y

حول	*ḥōl*	year
حولي	*ḥōli*	year old

Chapter Thirteen
SUBJECT VOCABULARIES

THE FOLLOWING lists give the specific names, or phrases used, in particular cases.

1 Agriculture

Many people are employed in Oman's agricultural sector. The following are some of the terms used:

(a) Dates

There are said to be over a hundred varieties in Oman, but the most commonly discussed are:

بطاش	*buṭṭāsh*	earliest dates on Batinah coast (red)
نقال	*nagāl*	earliest dates (generally yellow)
خنيزي	*khineizi*	dates following *nagal*
زبـد	*zabad*	high quality
خـلاص	*khalāṣ*	highest quality at peak season
جـبري	*jibri*	,,
هـلالي	*hilāli*	last dates of the season
خصاب	*khaṣāb*	,,
مبسلى	*mubsili*	type sometimes boiled before export
فرض	*farḍ*	type which do not deteriorate even if dipped in sea-water

(b) **Other crops**

جت	*jatt*	alfalfa (lucerne)
قت	*gatt*	,,
مشمش	*mishmish*	apricot
موز	*mōz*	banana
لوبية	*lūbya*	beans
مشلي	*mashli*	coconut (young)
جارز	*jāriz*	,, (older)
نارجيلة	*nārjīla*	,, (mature)
تين	*tīn*	figs
عنب	*'inab*	grape
زيتون	*zeitūn*	guava
لومي	*lūmi*	lime
سفرجل	*safarjil*	lime (sweet)
بطيخ	*baṭṭīkh*	melon
جح	*jiḥḥ*	melon (water)
فرصاد	*furṣād*	mulberry
برتقال	*burtagāl*	orange
فيفاي	*fīfāi*	pawpaw
خوخ	*khōkh*	peach
رمان	*rummān*	pomegranate
ذرة	*dhura*	sorghum
حنطة	*ḥunṭa*	wheat
بر	*burr*	,,

(c) Farming Terms

بستان	*bustān*	garden
نخل (نخيل)	*nakhl* (*nakhīl*)	palm(s)
جلبة	*jilba*	plot (for individual palms)
جيل	*jeil*	area of palms irrigated at one time
صرمة	*ṣarma*	very young palm
حارس	*ḥāris*	guardian of trees
بيدار	*bīdār*	farmer who ensures that trimming, pollinating and ploughing are done
عامل	*'āmil*	casual labourer
حيس القيظ	*ḥeis al-geiṭh*	spring ploughing
حيس الشتاء	*ḥeis ash-shitā*	winter ploughing
مغارسة	*mughārasa*	planting contract
مسقاة	*musgā*	watering (or contract)
مزارعة	*muzāra'a*	sowing (or contract)
غيل	*gheil*	cultivation from water lying in wadis
بكارة	*bakāra*	pulley over well
منجور	*manjūr*	,,
غراق	*gharrāg*	syphon (inside)
فلاح	*falāḥ*	,, (outside)

2 Animals (wild)

خنفس	*khunfus*	beetle
فهد	*fahd*	cheetah · leopard
ثعالب	*tha'lab*	fox
حصيني	*ḥuṣeini*	,,
ظبي	*ṭhabi*	gazelle
سافن	*sāfin*	hyrax
وعل	*wa'al*	ibex
طهه	*ṭaha*	Jayakar's goat

ظب	*ṭhubb*	lizard
وعل	*wa'al*	mountain goat
بن سولع	*bin sōli'*	oryx
ابو ريش	*abū rīsh*	porcupine
ذيب	*dhīb*	wolf

3 Birds

حبارى	*ḥubāra*	bustard
غراب	*ghurāb*	crow
بط	*buṭṭ*	duck
نسر	*nisr*	eagle
شاهين	*shāhīn*	hawk
حر	*ḥurr*	,,
ابو ناغور	*abu nāghūr*	heron
بنقور	*bangūr*	,,
صفرد	*ṣifrid*	partridge
حمام	*ḥamām*	pigeon
قطاة	*gaṭa*	sandgrouse
حويري	*ḥuweiri*	seagull
سويدي	*suweidi*	,,
فرخ	*farkh*	,,
عصفور	*'aṣfūr*	sparrow
رخمة	*rukhma*	vulture

4 Fish and Marine Life

The following are some of the more common words, although usage differs in the various parts of the area and there are many local variants:

سفيلة	*sufeila*	abilone
جد	*jad*	barracuda
بنت النوخذا	*bint in-nōkhdha*	captain's daughter
دوك	*dūk*	clam
زئو	*zi'u*	cowrie
قبقب	*gubgub*	crab

جوشن	*gūshin*	crab
دشن	*dishin*	,,
ام الربيان	*umm ar-ribyān*	crayfish
خارش بارش	*khārish bārish*	,,
شباس	*shibās*	,,
كرمباخ	*kurumbākh*	,,
شرخة	*sharkha*	,,
فش	*fesh*	cuttle fish
تنك	*tank*	,,
دغس	*dughus*	dolphin
ناخوت	*nākhūt*	eel (Moray)
مزف	*miziff*	,,
جار	*jār*	,,
جراد البحر	*jarād il-baḥr*	flying fish
خرخور	*kharkhūr*	garfish
حاقول	*ḥāgūl*	,,
كنعد	*kan'ad* (*pronounced chan'ad in the Gulf*)	mackerel (kingfish)
ظلعة	*ṭhal'a*	,, (queenfish)
دبس	*dibis*	,, (horse)
زئـو	*zi'u*	mollusc
جن	*jann*	parrot fish
خودير	*khaudīr*	,, ,,
لولوة (لولو)	*lūluwwa* (*pl. lūlū*)	pearl
قماش (قماشة)	*gumāsh* (*pl. gumāsha*)	pearls
غوص	*ghōṣ*	pearling
ربيان	*ribyān*	prawn (in the Gulf)
	shibās	,, (in Oman)
فقل	*fugl*	puffer fish
بقمة	*bugma*	,, ,,
طباق	*ṭabāg*	ray
شرس	*shurs*	,,
عنان	*'anān*	ray (electric)

حمرة	*ḥamra*	red snapper
هامور	*hāmūr*	rock cod (Garrupa)
عومة	*'ūma*	sardine
خيل	*kheil*	seahorse
جرجور	*jarjūr*	shark
لخمة	*lukhma*	,,
ابو القرون	*abu-l-gurūn*	shark (hammerhead)
اقلة	*agla*	snapper
جران	*jurān*	sole
ابو سيف	*abū seif*	swordfish (sawfish)
حمسة	*ḥimisa*	turtle
غيلمة	*gheilma*	,,
جرام	*jarām*	whale
جناز	*janāz*	whale shark
برية	*barriya*	whitebait

5 Food

Food varies considerably from place to place, but goat or mutton is the usual basis of the midday or evening meal, especially when formal hospitality is offered. The following are some of the words used in connection with meals:

خوزي	*khūzi*	mutton or goat served on mounded rice
مشكاك	*mushkāk*	kebab on skewer of palm
مشوي	*mashwi*	mutton or goat baked in an earth oven
مرق	*marag*	stewed mutton in pot
قبولي	*gubūli*	mutton on mound of rice
خبز	*khubz*	bread
خبز رقيق (رخال)	*khubz ragīg (rukhāl)*	bread (wafer thin)
عيش	*'eish*	rice
فوالة	*fowāla*	light meal
حلوى	*ḥalwa*	sweet (halwa)

6 Guns

The principal words used for guns and military items are:

تفكة وتفقة	*tafka, tafga*	gun (general)
تفك وتفكان (تفق وتفقان)	*tufuk, tufkān* (*tufug, tufgān*)	,, (plural)
ابو عشر	*abu 'ashar*	.303
سكتون	*saktūn*	.22
شوزن	*shōzun*	shotgun
صمع	*ṣumma'*	Martini Henry
ابو فتيلة	*abū fiteila*	long-barrelled matchlock
عصاني	*'uṣāni*	,,
رشاشة	*rashshāsha*	machine gun
مدفع الميدان	*madfa' al-meidān*	field gun
حاون	*hāwin*	mortar
عتاد	*'itād*	ammunition
فشكة	*fashka*	round
طلقة	*ṭalga*	,,
قصفة	*gaṣfa*	shell
قنبلة	*gunbula*	bomb
قنبلة يدوية	*gunbula yadawīya*	grenade
لغم	*laghm*	mine

7 Military Ranks

These vary to some extent from country to country but the following are the terms used in Oman:

لوا	*liwa*	Major General
عميد	*'amīd*	Brigadier
عقيد	*'agīd*	Colonel
مقدم	*mugaddam*	Lieutenant Colonel
رائد	*rā'id*	Major
نقيب (رئيس)	*nagīb* (*ra'īs*)	Captain
ملازم أول	*mulāzim awal*	Lieutenant
ملازم ثاني	*mulāzim thāni*	Second Lieutenant

طالب ضابط	*ṭālib ṭhabiṭ*	Officer Cadet
رئيس ركاب	*ra'īs rukāb*	Sergeant Major
نائب ضابط أول	*nā'ib ṭhabiṭ awal*	Warrant Officer I
نائب ضابط ثاني	*nā'ib ṭhābiṭ thani*	Warrant Officer II
رقيب معلم	*ragīb mu'allam*	Staff Sergeant
رقيب (شاويش)	*ragīb (shāwīsh)*	Sergeant
اريف	*'arīf*	Corporal
جندي اول	*jundi awwal*	Lance Corporal
جندي	*jundi*	soldier
جندي جديد	*jundi jadīd*	recruit

8 Omani Phrases

The following are a small number of characteristic phrases used in some parts of Oman:

ما أدري به *mā adri bu*	I do not know about that
وما ادري مو *wa mā adri mū*	And goodness knows what else
يفتكر باطن ان *yaftikir bāṭin an*	He really thinks that . . .
توني وصلت *tawni waṣalt*	I have just arrived
توه جاي *taww jāi*	He is just coming (in Oman this can also mean: he has just come)
ما اروم اقال لك *mā arūm agūl lik*	I would rather not tell you
ما قصرت *mā gaṣṣart*	You have not failed (fallen short)
شيُ ويوجد *shī, yujad*	There is (something)

شيء *shī*	There are (some)
ما عنده شجره *mā andu shajara*	He has no tree (*viz:* he is not a Bedu)
ما له اصل *mā lihu aṣil*	He has no roots: his story has no foundation
عبارة *'ibāra*	That is to say
ما يصير *mā yaṣīr*	It will not do *or* it cannot be
صار *sār*	It will be done (in response to a command)

9 Ships and Boats

There are many types of local craft. The more common names are given below. The word dhow, which is applied to all sorts of local craft by Europeans is never used. It was originally used to refer to a now extinct form of craft found on the East African Coast.

خشب	*khashab*	boat or dhow (general)
لنش	*linsh*	boat or dhow (with engine)
جلبوت	*jalbūt*	boat with upright stem and transom stern
بوم	*būm*	larger boat with beak prow and sharp stern
سمبوك	*sambūk*	pearling boat
بغلة	*baghala*	large high-pooped boat
غنجة	*ghanjā*	,, ,, ,,
بدن	*badan*	small high-pooped boat (partly sewn together instead of nailed)

شوعي	*shū'i*	small fishing boat (similar in shape to *sambuk*)
هوري	*hūri*	small dug-out or dinghy
عبرة	*'abra*	ferry
شحوف	*shahūf*	pram
شاشة	*shāsha*	palm-frond boat, found on Batinah Coast

The word used generically for a boat, small or large is:

سفينة (سفن)	*safina* (*sufun*)

The words used for large ships are:

منوة (منور)	*manwa* (*manwar*)	warship
بارجة	or *bārja*	,,
باخرة	*bākhira*	steamer
مركب	*markib*	ship (generally)
سفينة	or *safīna*	,,
حمالة النفط	*ḥimālat an-naft*	tanker
دوبة	*dūba*	barge

Terrain

The following are some of the principal sorts of terrain in the area:

وادي	*wādi*	dry valley
جبل	*jabal*	mountain
سيح	*sīḥ*	plain
حصى	*ḥaṣa*	rocky or stony area
سبخة	*sabkha*	saltmarsh
رمل	*raml*	sand dunes

11 Trees and Plants (Wild)

Trees

بوت	*būt*	coriander
لبان	*lubān*	frankincense
غاف	*ghāf*	ghaf (*Prosopis spicigera*)

علعلان	*'ala'lān*	juniper
نبق	*nabag*	nabag
نمت	*nimt*	nimt
اتم	*'atimm*	olive (wild)
سمرة	*samra*	samra (*Acacia ep*)
سدرة	*sidra*	sidra (*Zizyphus spinus*)
قرض	*garaḍ*	sunt
طلحة	*ṭalḥa*	talha (*Acacia Seyal Del.*)
جز	*jiz*	tamarisk
سوجر	*sōjur*	willow
سوير	*suweir*	,,

Plants

شحس	*shaḥas*	Dodonia
حشيش	*ḥashīsh*	grass
عشب	*'ishb*	,,
حرمل	*ḥarmil*	harmil (*Rhazya Stricta Decne*)
نيل	*nīl*	indigo
حبن	*ḥibin*	oleander
دفلى	*difla*	,,
رسل	*rasal*	reed
رمث	*rimth*	rimth (*Haloxylon Salicornicum* [*Moq.*] *Boiss*)

12 Winds

The names of the principal winds are:

شمال	*shamāl*	north wind (or a high wind from the north or west)
ازيب	*azyab*	north wind
بحري	*baḥri*	light north wind (from the sea)

سهيلي	*suheili*	south wind
بري	*barri*	light south wind in the early morning (from the land)
قوس (كوس)	*gōs* (*kōs*)	high east wind
نعشي	*na'shi*	light east wind
مطلعي	*muṭla'i*	strong south-east wind
غربـي	*gharbi*	west wind

Chapter Fourteen

OMANI PROVERBS

من غراب اربعين غراب
min ghurāb arba'īn ghurāb
From one crow, forty crows
cf "A mountain out of a molehill"

التجارب اكبر بيان والمستقبل كشاف
at-tajārib akbar biyān wa al-mustagbal kashshāf
Experience is the best proof and the future reveals (all)
cf "The proof of the pudding is in the eating"

بيضة اليوم ولا فرخ باكر
beiḍah al-yom wa lā farkh bākir
An egg today rather than a chicken tomorrow
cf "A bird in the hand is worth two in the bush"

لا تولي شؤونك غيرك
lā tawala shu'ūnak gheirak
No one looks after your affairs like yourself

ان الطيور على اشكالها تقع
innaṭ-ṭuyūr 'ala ashkālha tega'
cf "Birds of a feather flock together"

نوخذاين في السفينة تغرق
nōkhdhāein fi-s-safīnah taghrag
If there are two captains, the ship sinks

اذا تعدد قواد السفينة غرقت
idha t'addad guwwad as-safīnah ghuragat
If there are too many captains, the ship sinks
cf "Too many cooks spoil the broth"

ما يحك شفري الا ظفري

mā yaḥikk shafri illa ṭhafri

Only my own nail can scratch my lip

or

ما حك جلدك (ظهرك) مثل ظفرك

mā ḥakk jaldak (ṭhakrak) mithil ṭhafrak

No one can scratch your skin (back) like your own nail

انا اقول جمل وانت تقول جبل

ana agūl jamal wa anta tagūl jabal

I say a camel when you say a mountain

cf "We are poles apart"

ان كان نيتك عمار ما يضرك ضريط الحمار

in kān nīyatak 'umār mā yaḍurrak ḍarīṭ il-ḥumār

If your intentions are good a donkey breaking wind will not hurt you

cf "Do not be put off from doing good by little obstacles"

بو يخجل من بنت عمه ما يجيث اولاد

bū yakhjal min bint 'amuh mā yajīb aulād

He who is shy of his cousin produces no children

(*NB* A man is normally expected to marry his cousin in Oman and Arabia generally.)

cf "Faint heart never won fair lady"

بو ياكل حلواها يصبر على بلواها

bū yākil ḥalwāha yaṣbur 'ala balwāha

He who eats of her "halwa" (sweetmeat) must (also) put up with her misfortune

cf "One must take the rough with the smooth"

بو يضرب عمره ما يبكي
bū yaḍrub 'amruh mā yabki
He who beats himself does not (has no right to) cry
cf "He brought it on himself"

بو ما يعرفك ما يثمنك
bū mā ya'rufak mā yathmanak
He who does not know you does not value you
cf "Out of sight: out of mind"

البيت يدخل من بابه
al-beit yudkhal min bābuh
The house is entered by its door
cf "There is a right and wrong way of doing things"

بين الاحباب تسقط الاداب
bein al-aḥbāb tasqaṭ al-ādāb
Between friends ceremony is dropped
cf "Do not stand on ceremony"

الجرف الملدوغ منه لا تدخل يدك فيه مرة ثانية
al-jarf al-maldūgh minnu lā tadakhkhal yiddak marra thānya
cf "Once bitten, twice shy"

جلد فار ما يستوي منه طبل
jild fār mā yistuwi minnuh ṭabil
A drum cannot be made from a rat's skin
cf "Silk purse/sow's ear"

الخابورة مخبورة
al-Khābūrah makhbūrah
Khābūrah (a town on the Bātinah Coast) is well known
cf "Queen Anne is dead"

خنفساءنا في عين امها غزالة
khunfusāna fī 'ein ummha ghazāla
Our black beetle is a gazelle in its mother's eyes
(*NB* "Khunfus" is the word for *Adesmia cothurnata.*)
cf "All her geese are swans"

الخير في بطن الشر
al-kheir fī baṭin ash-sharr
Good is in the belly of evil
cf "Every cloud has a silver lining" and
"May something good come of it"

اركب الهزيلة لتلحق السمينة
irkab al-hazīlah li-talḥaq as-samīnah
Ride the lean (she camel) to catch up with the fat one
cf "Make the most of your opportunities"

صغارهم فلفل وكبارهم زنجبيل (جنزبيل)
ṣughārhum filfil wa kubārhum zanjubīl (*or janzubīl*)
Their little ones are pepper and their elders ginger

ضربني وبكى سبقني واشتكا
ḍarabni wa baka sabagnī wa shtaka
He hit me and wept; jumped the queue and complained
cf "He started the whole thing"

ضم مالك ولا تتهم جارك
ḍum malak wa lā tutahhim jārak
Look after your own things and do not accuse your neighbour
(of stealing them)
cf "Mind your own business"

يوم اسلم انا وناقتي ما على من رفاقتي
yōm aslam ana wa nāgati mā 'alei min rifāgati
When I and my camel are safe, I don't worry about my companions
cf "I'm all right, Jack"

طالع من الموت تاه في حضرموت
ṭāli' min al-mōt tāh fī Ḥaḍhramūt
Escaping from death he got lost in the Hadhramaut
cf "Out of the frying pan into the fire"

عند الحصايد يروم القصايد
'ind al-ḥaṣāid yarūm al-gaṣāid
At harvest times he goes around singing songs
cf "He is never there when he is wanted"

العطشانة تكسر الحوض

al-'aṭshānah taksir al-hōḍ
The thirsty (she camel) breaks the drinking trough
cf "Necessity knows no law"

غابت السكرة وجات الفكرة

ghābat as-sikra wa jāt al-fikra
Drunkenness has gone and consciousness has come
cf "He has come to his senses"

بو يبغي يصلي يندلها القبلة

bū yabghi yuṣalli yindallha al-qibla
He who wants to pray needs no guide to face Mecca

كان تبغي تصلي ما تغلب

kān tabghi tuṣallī mā tughlab
If you want to pray, you cannot be prevented
cf "Where there's a will there's a way"

كبره كبر نخلة وعقله عقل سخلة

kubruh kubr nakhluh wa 'agluh 'agl sakhluh
He is as big as his date trees but only as wise as his kids
cf "He is all brawn and no brain"

كثير في العزاف غم في البطن

kathīr fī al-'azāf ghumm fī al-baṭin
Plenty on the table but sadness in the stomach
cf "Poverty amidst plenty"

كف واحد ما يسفق

kaff wāḥid mā yasaffig
One hand cannot applaud by itself
cf "You can't do it alone"

كل حله فيها عله

kull ḥilla fīhā 'illa
Every village has some drawback
cf "There's a black side to everything" and
"Every family has its skeleton in the cupboard"

كل ذنبه على جنبه

kull dhanbu 'ala janbu

All his crimes are his own responsibility

cf "On your head be it"

كما قصاب نزوى

kama gaṣṣāb Nizwa

Like a butcher of Nizwa (*NB* The butchers of Nizwa were noted for complaining about suffering a loss when they had done quite well.)

cf "A British farmer!"

لا تأمن من الثور ولو رأسه في التنور

lā tāmin min al-thōr walū rāsuk fi-tannūr

Do not trust a bull even though its head is in the oven

cf "The hare and the tortoise"

لي يدخل بين البصل والثوم يطلع خايس ومذموم

la yadkhul bein al-baṣal wa al-thūm yaṭla' khāis wa madhmūm

He who goes amongst onion and garlic comes out stinking

cf "The dirt will rub off on him" *or* "He will get his fingers burnt"

ما بادل المحبوب الحشاجني

mā bādil al-maḥbūb al-ḥashā jinnī

One does not exchange a sweetheart for a Jinni (evil spirit)

cf "Do not throw away your all"

contrast "Fair exchange is no robbery"

ما رام السيل يسكب الحصى رطب

mā rām as-seil yaskib al-ḥaṣa ruṭub

As long as the flood continues the stones remain wet

cf "Make hay while the sun shines"

ما على الكريم تشترط

mā 'ala al-karīm tasharruṭ

No conditions can be imposed on the generous

cf "Be thankful for small mercies"

من طمع طبع

min ṭama' ṭaba'

From covetousness drowning

cf "Greed was his downfall"

من غاب عن العين غاب عن القلب

man ghāb 'an al-'ein ghāb 'an al-qalb

He who is out of sight is absent from the heart

cf "Out of sight, out of mind"

النار تخلف رماد

an-nār takhallif rumād

Fire leaves ashes behind

cf "He is not the man his father was"

نار السمر تخلف جمر

nār as-samur takhallif al-jamur

The fire of the *samr* tree (acacia) leaves cinders

cf "A chip off the old block"

contrast "It's all dust and ashes"

يا سارق الديك فوق راسك الريش

yā sāriq ad-dīk fōg rāsak ar-rīsh

Oh thief of the cock the feather is on your head

cf "Your sins will find you out" and "His guilt was written on his face"

يا غريب كون اديب

yā gharīb kūn adīb

Oh stranger, be well behaved

cf "When in Rome . . ."

اربط الحمار مع الحصان يتعلم من طبعه

irbaṭ al-ḥimār mā al-ḥuṣān yat'allam min ṭab'uh

Tie up the ass with the horse and he will learn from following him

رابع الكذاب الى رز الباب

rābi 'al-kadhdhāb ila razz al-bāb

Accompany the liar to the lintel of the door

cf "Do not let the Devil cross the threshold" and

"Give him the benefit of the doubt"

بعد العود ما شئ قعود

ba'ad al-'ūd mā shī gu'ūd

After the incense (is served) there is no sitting on

العود حتى تعود

al-'ūd ḥatta ta'ūd

Incense so that you come back.